Jonas Brothers
Hello Beautiful

POSY EDWARDS

Introducing The Jonas Brothers

*W*hat an amazing year for the Jonas Brothers! Kevin, Joe and Nick are three pretty special boys. They've been playing guitars, singing and performing since they could walk. Now they are set to seize the limelight, starring in the smash-hit Disney movie, *Camp Rock!*

These boys from Wyckoff, New Jersey, have certainly worked hard and have come a long way from their humble beginnings performing in a church band. They have written and released three albums and have played live alongside the likes of Avril Lavigne, Kelly Clarkson, Corbin Bleu and Good Charlotte. But music is not all that these talented boys are up to. As well as *Camp Rock!* there is a TV series in the pipeline and who knows what other opportunities await them.

They've won hearts across the globe, and it's not hard to see why. They are blessed with musical talent and write songs about their own experiences of love and heartbreak. These boys also definitely have the looks – their signature brown eyes and unkempt brown hair have melted the hearts of thousands of fans all over the world!

But don't start thinking that the Jonas Brothers have let all this success go to their heads – far from it. They're modest about their achievements; in fact, these three boys are as down-to-earth as they come. They play pranks on each other, do chores around the house (or the tour bus!) and help their parents out. It's a good job they have so much energy, as it looks like they're going to be in huge demand over the coming years!

5

KEVIN JONAS

'One of my biggest pet peeves is when my brothers tell me how to drive. It just freaks me out because they've never been behind the wheel before.'
Kevin

You could say that the Jonas Brothers started all the way back when Kevin was ill and stayed home from school one day. He picked up a 'teach yourself guitar' book and taught himself how to play. He even faked being sick the next day so he could stay home and practise! But we're sure mum Denise couldn't be that mad at him for it – just look where it's got him!

Of course, that doesn't mean he's a bad kid. Being the oldest, Kevin does everything his parents ask him to do and tries to help as much as possible. And with three younger brothers, his parents probably need a little help sometimes! Kevin is very protective of his younger brothers and gives Joe, Nick or Frankie advice when they face a new and tough situation – Kevin's almost certainly faced it before!

Kevin Jonas fact file

Full name: Paul Kevin Jonas II
Nicknames: K2 and Sherlock (because he talks about subjects as if he knows everything about them!)
Birthday: 5 November 1987
Born in: Teaneck, New Jersey, USA
Current location: Hollywood, California, USA
Star sign: Scorpio
Chinese horoscope sign: Rabbit
Favourite colour: Green
Favourite song: '3x5' by John Mayer
Favourite bands: John Mayer and Switchfoot
Hobbies: Playing guitar, bowling
Favourite actresses: Rachel McAdams and Hayden Panettiere
Favourite actor: James Dean
Favourite movies: The *High School Musical* movies and *About a Boy*
Favourite TV Shows: *Heroes, Close To Home, Lost* and *Jack and Bobby*
Favourite word: 'Excellent'
Ringtone: 'Good Life' by Kanye West featuring T-Pain
Biggest fear: Disappointing people he cares about
Favourite food: Sushi, Italian, Thai and his mother's cheese lasagne
Favourite ice cream: Rocky Road
Favourite drink: Kevin has a serious Starbucks obsession. He likes Mocha frappuccinos when it's hot outside, or Chai latte with extra chai, no water and skimmed milk
Food hate: Fruit
Hidden talents: Kevin is good at skateboarding and ping-pong. He is also double jointed and can burp on command!
Obsession: MacBook (all the brothers have their own, with wireless built in)

Kevin Jonas-isms

Kevin has freckles in the shape of a star on his neck.

Kids used to tease Kevin about having Spock ears.

Kevin had no teeth in the first grade.

Growing up Kevin wanted to be a cowboy.

Kevin has a yellow toothbrush.

Kevin can't go to sleep without making his bed first. Even if it's been made in the morning, he has to remake it! It's his quirky habit. Kevin never has any trouble sleeping but he loves to stay up late. Luckily for him, younger brother Joe – whom he shares a room with – likes staying up late too! But if there's one thing that Kevin is, it's messy, according to roomie Joe. 'On the tour bus, Kevin's bunk was above mine and somehow all his stuff would end up in my bunk! I would tell him to get it out of my bunk and then he'd just put it on the floor.' It's a good job for Kevin his brother is so easy-going and laid back!

JOE JONAS

According to his mum, Joe was quiet as a child, but he's certainly outgrown that now, as the self-proclaimed loudest, messiest and laziest Jonas brother! Growing up, Joe describes himself as a weird kid. He used to think it was cool to go to bed and pretend to fall asleep, then get up and change into his school clothes for the next day and sleep in them!

When Joe was younger he never thought about singing, instead he thought he would like to be a comedian, but like his brothers, he still sang in the church choir. And after performing in three Broadway productions, it became clear he had talent in other areas too. Today Joe is best known for his random sayings and his crazy dances ... oh yeah – and also for playing the lead in the hot Disney movie, *Camp Rock!*

'When he was younger, Joe would do things like getting his head stuck in between bars of a railing and it would take firemen to get him out.'
Mum, Denise Jonas

Joe Jonas-isms

'If I could have a superpower, I would probably want to be able to shoot spaghetti out of my fingers.'

'One thing nobody knows about me is that three of my fingers are edible, but I can't tell you which fingers.'

'If I had to be a crayon, I would be the colour orange, black, white, dot, clear, red.'

'Every studio needs a rubber chicken.'

Once, when Joe was a kid, he got his head stuck in his tambourine. He hasn't outgrown being accident-prone either – in January 2008 Joe was rushed to the hospital when he tripped on a grate backstage at an Atlantic City concert, where he and his brothers were making a video for YouTube. Joe received stitches for his head injury, but luckily it was nothing serious. Phew!

The Jonas household only had one pet, Joe's dog Cocoa. When Cocoa passed away in 2007, the boys were on the *Best of Both Worlds* tour. 'I definitely teared up when I heard about Cocoa,' he says. 'Cocoa was my dog, I picked him when I was five!' To date, Joe isn't sure whether he'll get another dog. His favourite animals are kangaroos and monkeys, and being a real nature lover, Joe has some ambitious plans: his New Year's resolution is to learn how to talk to animals!

Joe Jonas fact file

Full name: Joseph Adam Jonas
Nicknames: Joe, JJ, DJ Danger
Birthday: 15 August 1989
Born in: Casa Grande, Arizona, USA
Current location: Hollywood, California, USA
Star sign: Leo
Chinese horoscope sign: Snake
Favourite colour: Blue
Favourite song: 'Only Hope' by Switchfoot
Favourite bands: Copeland and Switchfoot
Hobbies: Making movies, jogging and working out
Joe can't live without: His iPhone. He's always using it
Favourite actress: Natalie Portman
Favourite actors: Jim Carrey and Johnny Depp
Favourite movies: The *High School Musical* movies, also *School for Scoundrels* and *Dumb and Dumber*
Favourite TV shows: *Boy Meets World*, *Heroes*, *Lost* and *Friends*
Ringtone: 'Can I Get Get Get' by Junior Senior
Favourite food: Any kind of exotic food, his grandma's homemade pizza, organic peanut butter with red apples
Favourite sweet snack: An Aero (a British favourite)
Favourite drink: Orange Gatorade, Red Bull, chocolate milk and water
First holiday: Mexico, though his favourite holiday spots are the Bahamas and Jamaica
Bad habit: Biting his nails
Biggest splurge: He bought an old-school Schwinn bike. Joe, his brothers and their friend Maya are always going for bike rides

Nick Jonas-isms

According to mum Denise, Nick will 'only eat his hamburgers in circles. He goes around the outside instead of digging right through!'

The first song Nick ever sang was from *Peter Pan*.

Nick says he spends too much money in the iTunes store.

NICK JONAS

'Nick is in charge – he's the youngest but he's definitely the boss. Everyone says he's shy because he's quiet, but he's not shy. He's Mr Cool!'
Kevin

The youngest member of the band (but not the youngest real-life Jonas brother), Nick Jonas describes himself as the quietest guy in the bunch. But don't be fooled: Nick's always loved the limelight, and has been singing since he was two and performing since he was three. He was a very creative and independent child, but he still gets upset when things go wrong or when he doesn't do well. He says he used to be very uptight, but he's learning to loosen up.

And with such great brothers, it's no wonder! 'Even though me and my older brothers have a younger brother, I'm considered the baby. But I'm more adult than Joe and Kevin!' he says. 'A lot of people have families where it's the younger kids that get all the slack, but they really do treat me with respect and I do the same for them, so it's a good relationship.' Nick says the main thing that makes him laugh is when his brothers goof around, but he hates it when they take his stuff. Nick shares a bedroom with his younger brother Frankie, and he keeps his closet surprisingly clean!

'On the way to the hospital Kevin and Joe looked up diabetes online. They knew more about it than I did before I got there! They're there for me all the time!'
Nick

Diabetes shock

In November 2005, Nick Jonas found out that he had Type 1 diabetes. A couple of months before he was diagnosed, he began to notice he was losing weight, developed a bad attitude, was constantly thirsty and always going to the bathroom. Nick took time off the tour to see a doctor, who sent him to hospital immediately. He's managing fine these days, and is hopeful that a cure will be discovered one day. In the meantime he's busy providing inspiration for kids who suffer from diabetes. 'Don't let it slow you down at all,' is his message. 'Just keep a positive attitude and keep moving forward with it! Don't be discouraged.'

Nick Jonas fact file

Full name: Nicholas Jerry Jonas
Nicknames: Nick J and Mr President (because he always acts like the boss)
Birthday: 16 September 1992
Born in: Dallas, Texas, USA
Current location: Hollywood, California, USA
Star sign: Virgo
Chinese horoscope sign: Monkey
Favourite colour: Blue
Favourite song: 'Superstition' by Stevie Wonder
Favourite bands: Switchfoot, Fall Out Boy, Maroon 5, Johnny Cash, The Animals, and The Rascals
Hobbies: Music, songwriting, baseball, collecting baseball cards, tennis
Favourite actress: Keri Lynn Pratt from *Jack and Bobby*
Favourite actor: Matt Long from *Jack and Bobby*
Favourite movie: *Finding Neverland*
Favourite TV shows: *Lost* and *Heroes*
Ringtone: 'Abracadabra' by The Steve Miller Band
Hidden talents: Playing the drums, breakdancing, one-handed cartwheels and making really good macaroni cheese
Health fact: Nick's eyes are supersensitive to light
Sleep fact: Nick can fall asleep in the most uncomfortable positions
Most ticklish spot: Feet
Favourite pastime: Reading
First major purchase: Gameboy Advance
Favourite food: Steak and his mother's egg casserole dish for breakfast

The Band: Background

Although the band are now releasing their third studio album, and are set to conquer the world with their TV and movie outings, the Jonas Brothers almost didn't make it this far.

TALENTED TODDLERS

When Nick Jonas was a toddler, he would stand on an improvised stage he had made from the coffee table, singing his heart out into a turkey baster! His grandma, 'Mama Fran', told him off, but he said that he needed to practise – because he was going to be on Broadway.

Dad Kevin used to teach songwriting at a bible college, and he also wrote and recorded Christian music. Mum Denise was a singer who worked in the school registrar's office. They would take Christian singing groups on the road, and took the boys with them when they travelled! When they were at home, the three brothers would hang around the family piano for hours, making up songs.

THE JONAS BROTHERS

The band started as Nick's solo project. Nick, who shares lead vocals with Joe in the band, began singing as soon as he could talk. His voice (that people often compare to Stevie Wonder's) was 'discovered' when he was singing while getting his hair cut in a local barbershop. He caught the attention of a woman in the shop who immediately referred him to a professional showbusiness manager. That was when he was just a tiny six-year-old!

At age seven, Nick began performing in musicals on Broadway. In 2002, while performing in *Beauty and the Beast*, Nick wrote a Christmas song with his father, which was released as a single and quickly became popular. In 2004, a second single was released, followed by a solo album that Nick, along with Kevin and Joe, had written several other songs for. While Nick was working on his solo project, Joe followed in his footsteps and performed on Broadway too.

In 2005, the new president of Columbia Records listened to Nick's record and really liked his voice. After meeting with Nick and hearing the song 'Please Be Mine', written and performed by all three brothers, Columbia Records decided to sign them as a group act.

Jonas Family fact

When Kevin was 16 he would travel around New York on his own, auditioning for bands and commercials.

FINDING A NAME

After being signed to Columbia, the brothers thought about calling themselves Sons of Jonas, but finally decided on the name Jonas Brothers. They toured in 2005 and started work on their album *It's About Time*, which was supposed to be released in February 2006, but was pushed back several times, finally coming out in August 2006.

'I used to play the drums in our church bands and I wasn't very good. To be playing in front of so many people now is amazing!'
Nick

Because their label didn't seem interested in promoting them, the Jonas Brothers considered switching labels. Despite Nick's solo single being re-released, the boys touring again with teen pop duo Aly and AJ Michalka, and the single 'Year 3000' becoming a hit on Radio Disney, the Jonas Brothers were finally dropped by their label in January 2007, much to the dismay of their fan base.

But thankfully they didn't stay without a label for long. The Jonas Brothers soon signed with Hollywood Records and began singing jingles for commercials. They worked on a new album, called *Jonas Brothers*, which was released later that year, and they also made a whole host of television and live appearances.

Jonas Family fact

When the family moved to New Jersey, Nick would put on his own shows in the basement, making tickets from construction paper and selling them for $5 each! Often the performances included singing and dancing, mostly to the music of boy bands like the Backstreet Boys and *NSYNC.

BUSY BROTHERS!

So far 2008 has seen them on their first headline US tour, as well as opening for the Avril Lavigne European tour. And, as if things couldn't get any better, there is a third album (*A Little Bit Longer*), another headline tour (the *Burning Up* tour), a TV series (*J.O.N.A.S!*) as well as their first movie for the Disney Channel: *Camp Rock!* in the pipeline. How do they fit it all in?!

Family and School Report

HOME LIFE

Two people the Jonas Brothers are always giving respect to are their parents: Paul Kevin Jonas Senior and Denise Jonas. Dad is an ordained minister, who met mum Denise in a church singing group in their hometown of Wyckoff, New Jersey, where Denise was a sign-language teacher. Both parents are musicians, so music played a major part in the Jonas brothers' lives while they were growing up. Can you imagine all the singing around the piano at Christmas?!

At home, the boys live ordinary teenage lives. 'We have to listen to our parents, just like any other kids. We do normal teenager stuff; we have to take out the trash. We do the same kind of stuff that everyone does,' says Nick. He also has the added chore of keeping an eye on Frankie when they're packing for going on tour (otherwise Frankie would bring nothing but toys!).

And in case you think Nick isn't telling the truth, his dad backs him up. 'These boys are rock stars, but they still do chores. It's just that their house is a bus! You can't cut the grass but you still have to make your bed and clean up after yourself.' Don't think that just because they're in a rock band, these boys are excused from helping out. In fact, their everyday life is probably pretty similar to your own!

School Report: Kevin

Favourite subjects: History and Latin, Physical Science and Chemistry

Favourite things about school: Pole vaulting and the social aspect

Favourite historical era: The Dark Ages

Least favourite thing about school: Waking up so early

If he went to college, he'd probably major in: Music or Engineering

Frankie 'Bonus Jonas' Facts

Birthday: 28 September 2000
Current home: LA, California, USA
Favourite holiday: Christmas
Favourite colours: Red-orange and green
Favourite show: *The Suite Life of Zack and Cody*

Today the Jonas brothers' mum and dad have taken on the role of managers, and the whole family travels around together on tour, sometimes with the grandparents too. Nick describes his parents as his biggest influence: 'They are totally amazing people that I'm blessed to have in my life.' The boys are also renowned for treating their favourite lady right: their mum! She doesn't ask for much from her boys (she only asked for sunglasses for Mother's Day!), but they're always treating her to sweet things, like breakfast in bed.

Mum Denise says her boys are 'so, so gracious. They really are attentive to me, which I have to be thankful for, because I know there are guys who don't pay attention. They're always checking on me, seeing if I'm okay.' The brothers treated their mother to lunch on Mother's Day, and took her out on her birthday too. These three hotties have obviously been brought up right!

BONUS JONAS

While Nick, Joe and Kevin are the brothers you might see hogging the limelight, they have another less famous sibling: their little brother, Frankie. Frank the Tank, or Bonus Jonas as he's often called, was born in the boys' hometown of Wyckoff, New Jersey. He has dark hair and brown eyes just like his older brothers. Joe was so excited when his younger brother Frankie was born that the first night Frankie was home from the hospital, Joe woke up to help his mother with feeding and nappy-changing. What a great brother!

While he might not be an official part of the Jonas Brothers band, Bonus Jonas has an equal share of musical talent. He knows how to play the guitar, and wants to learn to play

Favourite subjects: Spelling and Geology

Favourite thing about school: Learning new information

Favourite historical era: The French Revolution

Least favourite subject: Mathematics

If he went to college, he'd probably major in: Music (although if the band continues to be successful he doesn't think he'll go to college)

drums too. His older brothers asked him if he wanted to be in their band, but he said he was going to start one of his own, which he did! Frankie's band is called Drop/Slap and he has no plans to join his brothers' band when he gets older. His favourite song is 'That's Just The Way We Roll' from the *Jonas Brothers* album.

Although he's yet to achieve the superstardom of his brothers, Frankie already has celebrity friends – he video-chats with Miley Cyrus's little sister, Noah. And speaking of Miley Cyrus, the *Hannah Montana* star is Frankie's secret celebrity crush! His older brother Nick once said that he thought Miley was cute, and Frankie jokingly tried to beat him up. Bless him!

SCHOOL REPORT!

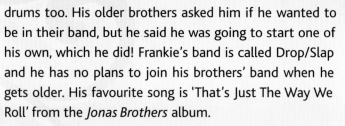

Due to the Jonas Brothers' hectic touring schedule, all three members have been home-schooled at some point. Kevin and Joe originally attended Eastern Christian High School in North Haledon, New Jersey. Kevin was home-schooled after his second year in high school, while Joe was in the seventh grade and Nick has always been home-schooled. But they still have their likes and dislikes when it comes to schoolwork, and come across the regular things that affect kids, like bullying. Nick says: 'I thought the popular kids were the cool kids. I got caught up in that, and it was bogus. High school is about finding who you are because that's more important than trying to be someone else.'

Favourite subjects: Mathematics, Physics and Social Science

Favourite thing about school: His desk

Favourite historical era: 1980s

If he went to college, he'd probably major in: Theatre Arts

'If bullies see that they're not affecting you, it won't be fun for them.'
Joe

Albums
Touring, Fans, Rumours

ALBUMS

It's About Time was the first studio album by the Jonas Brothers, released on 8 August 2006. It reached number 91 in the US Billboard chart, and there were two singles released from it: 'Mandy' and 'Year 3000'. To date, the album has sold over 50,000 copies worldwide! The Jonas Brothers' pop-punk style also featured uplifting, positive lyrics, showing that there was more to this band of brothers than your typical boy band.

Inspiration for the songs came directly from the boys' personal experiences, from the highs and lows of dating, to being on the road and following their dreams at such a young age.

What's in a name?

'We decided to call the album *It's About Time* because so many of our songs seem to deal with different aspects of time,' says Nick. Kevin explains that '6 Minutes' is about how quickly you can run through the full range of emotions when you feel strongly about someone you've just met, and '7:05' is about etching in your memory the exact time a relationship ended.

The single 'Mandy' tells the story about a girl who their mum Denise (a sign-language teacher) taught to sign so she could pursue her dream of working with the hearing-impaired.

Who Does What

Kevin Jonas – guitar, vocals

Joe Jonas – vocals, percussion, guitar, keyboards

Nick Jonas – vocals, guitar, piano, drums

'I'd have to say 'Year 3000' is my favourite song from *It's About Time* because it's just the one everyone knows and loves to hear.'
Kevin

> 'A lot of it is about typical teenage love stuff like "Oh, what am I going to do if I can't see her today?" It's not stuff that we don't know about.'
> Nick

JONAS BROTHERS

All three Jonas Brothers formed special friendships with Mandy – she even dated Joe for a while, and although the couple broke up they still remain good friends.

Other songs on the album that stand out for the boys include 'Time For Me To Fly', a catchy, fast track that is about following their dream of making music through hard work and trying to make things happen, and 'Don't Tell Anyone', one of the more emotional songs, which is about liking someone but not being able to admit it.

One thing the boys have always been admired for by their peers is their lyrical content. Nick says: 'In the moment, I'll have a strong inspiration for lyrics, and most of the time I really want to get it off my chest and let it go, whereas other people might write it down in a journal and be done with it or vent and get it out. I like to do that, but with songwriting, I'll just wanna write it. Most of the time, songs that come out of it are really cool.'

Jonas Brothers (2007)

Despite being dropped by their label after releasing *It's About Time*, the Jonas Brothers were soon signed by Hollywood Records, who recognised their talent. The boys released their second album, simply called *Jonas Brothers*, on this label. Kevin, Joe and Nick co-wrote all the songs, and their producer was John Fields, who also works with Switchfoot and Pink among others. He is an 'awesome producer' according to Kevin. The band worked really hard with John in the studio for 21 days straight. Phew!

Released in America on 7 August 2007, *Jonas Brothers* reached number five in the American chart, and went on to chart at number three in Mexico, number 43 in Australia and number 18 in the World Chart.

Three singles were also released – 'Hold On', 'SOS' (which was written by Nick in ten minutes after a bad break-up) and 'When You Look Me in the Eyes', although in Europe only 'SOS' was released. To date, the album has sold an awesome 1.4 million copies worldwide – that's a lot of Jonas fans!

According to Kevin, all the lyrics on the *Jonas Brothers* album were written from personal experiences. 'Relationships, good times, bad times and everything in between. Everything we went through in the year and a half before the album came out, we wrote about it. That makes us happy, it's our stuff, that's why we self-titled it, because it was a new introduction and a welcome back to us, explaining us a little better.'

And The Winner Is ...

It's not just the fans that love the Jonas Brothers – the band has also started receiving nominations and awards!

Awards:

Nickelodeon's Kids' Choice Award 2008: Favourite Music Group

★ ★ *Winner* ★ ★

What Perez Sez on VH1: Hottest Teen Sensation of 2007

★ ★ *Winner* ★ ★

Nominations:

Poptastic! Awards 2008

'The album is meant to get people up and have fun and raise their energy.'
Joe

'The lyrical content has gotten a little more in-depth as far as who we are as people and our personal lives, with our dating and all that, things we've gone through in the past year. We were really able to put it into the songs and make a really cool record.'
Nick on *A Little Bit Longer*

A Little Bit Longer (2008)

Despite all the touring, TV appearances and film debuts, somehow the Jonas Brothers found time to write their third studio album, *A Little Bit Longer*, released in August 2008. The album is named after the song 'A Little Bit Longer', which is a song that Nick wrote about dealing with diabetes. John Fields again produced it (although Timbaland is rumoured to have been involved too!), and the album features the hit single, 'Burning Up'.

Much of the album was recorded on the tour bus while the band was on the road, opening for Miley Cyrus on the sold-out Hannah Montana *Best of Both Worlds* tour. Nick says that a couple of guitar and bass tracks got recorded on the bus while it was actually rolling! When the tour ended, the boys got together in a proper LA studio to finish it off. Nick says that the album has the same Jonas Brothers sound, but with more influences: Elvis Costello, The Animals, The Rascals and The Beatles.

Both Kevin and Nick's favourite song from the album is 'Can't Have You'. All the brothers are really proud of their vocal chemistry. Joe says that Nick has the powerhouse vocal, with a young, soulful voice that catches everyone's ear.

TOURING

Performing at their local church sure gave the boys a good grounding for their future career! The real fun began when they combined their musical abilities by starting to write music and performing it on stage. The Jonas Brothers' first tour in 2005 saw them opening for Kelly Clarkson, Jesse McCartney, the Backstreet Boys and the Click Five. They spent the later portion of the year on an anti-drug tour with Aly & AJ Michalka and The Cheetah Girls. They also opened for The Veronicas in early 2006, promoting their album *It's About Time*. A pretty busy schedule for anyone, never mind three teenage boys from New Jersey! These days, when the boys tour, it's a family affair: mum, dad and little brother Frankie all go together, while Grandma goes along to help with the catering!

What a Marvellous Party

In early 2007 the Jonas Brothers began their *Marvellous Party* tour, which had a totally fabulous theme: that of a school prom! As the boys never got to go to their prom, they thought it would be awesome to bring the theme to their fans, live in concert. The tour contained photo booths to make it seem more realistic, just like an actual prom! And each of the Jonas Brothers has their own part to play on stage. 'Joe has this really cool, smooth rock voice,' says Nick. 'He really knows how to get the crowd going. Kevin is the one that holds us all together. Joe and I are the singers and we take turns on keyboards and percussion, but Kevin mostly plays the guitar and that's the part of the group that we need – he's the glue that keeps it together.'

Best of Both Worlds tour trivia

During the *Best of Both Worlds* tour, Joe would battle Miley on stage, doing microphone tricks in front of everyone to see who was the best! One time they were battling when Joe went down into a full split then came back up with his mic stand! Miley's mouth dropped! What a talent.

'I would be a good tour manager. I'm always asking the tour manager questions about how the tour runs.'
Kevin

Tour Bus Trivia

To get pumped before a show, the boys have a dance party on the tour bus. They have TVs and an enormous sound system, and they turn up everything as loud as it can possibly go. They crank it up and the bus is just rocking!

Best of Both Worlds

From 18 October 2007 to 9 January 2008, the Jonas Brothers opened for Miley Cyrus on her *Best of Both Worlds* tour. Kevin, Joe and Nick played 54 huge dates with Miley across the United States, warming up the crowds of screaming girls for the Miley/Hannah extravaganza, and also earning themselves some new fans in the meantime!

You might think the boys would get worn out from performing so much, but they have the perfect way to relax after a show. Nick says: 'It's about 11:30 by the time we get done. We all get back to the hotel and order cheeseburgers and play videogames like *Halo*. We'll order room service like four times. Then we'll be like "We need some ice-cream!"'

There were a few milestones reached on the *Best of Both Worlds* tour. One that was particularly special was Kevin turning the grand age of 20! To celebrate, the boys had a birthday party on the tour bus and invited everyone working on the tour. They had pizza, ice-cream cake, cheesecake, and they turned up the music – but Miley couldn't come because she was grounded!

Look Me in the Eyes

Being on the road with Miley was a great warm-up for the Jonas Brothers' first headline shows: the *Look Me in the Eyes* tour. This kicked off on 31 January 2008 in Arizona and finished on 22 March in the band's home state of New Jersey. At the end of the last show, the Jonas Brothers brought their family, friends, the opening bands and crew members from the tour out on stage and sang Queen's 'We Are the Champions'. Rooney opened every show for the boys, except when Valora or Menudo opened on a few select nights. During their shows,

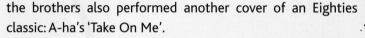

the brothers also performed another cover of an Eighties classic: A-ha's 'Take On Me'.

Goodness knows how they find the time for everything – in 2008 the Jonas Brothers opened for Avril Lavigne on the second leg of her European tour, and will be wowing fans with their *Burning Up* tour starting on 4 July in Toronto. On this tour they'll be playing loads of new material from their third album, *A Little Bit Longer*. One thing is for sure – the Jonas Brothers are psyched to keep the momentum going strong. 'We go crazy on stage!' says Kevin; 'It's so much fun!'

UK Visit

On their recent tour, the brothers visited the UK, where they wandered through London and had their first encounter with double-decker buses and old-fashioned red phone boxes ('very cool', according to Kevin). They also tried to raise a smile from the guards outside Buckingham Palace, but didn't succeed. The brothers went on the London Eye, then hit the West End to watch a production of *Les Misérables* – a musical they performed in back home! They also sampled some of the local cuisine: Joe says that 'the meat pies were amazing, but we won't be eating jellied eels again anytime soon!'

Favourites

When on stage, Kevin's favourite songs to play are 'I Am What I Am' and 'SOS'.

Nick likes to rock out to 'Year 3000' and 'Hollywood'.

In concert, Joe's favourite song to play is 'Still in Love With You'.

'Singing is hard work – it gets tiring, but, you know, when you get back on that stage, it's worth every bit. Every bit of energy that you spent to get there, it's completely worth it.'
Joe

29

FANS AND STARDOM

You would think it might get tiring not being able to walk down the street without getting chased by screaming girls, but the Jonas Brothers take it all in a day's work, because they love what they do. Joe says that sometimes when fans see him and his brothers they freak out, but he's as cool as a cucumber and says it's not really a big deal.

In fact, this Jonas brother is so laid-back and easy-going he even likes to play pranks on his fans! 'I walked up to two girls in an airport looking at *Popstar!* magazine and they had it opened at a page with me, Kevin and Nick on it,' says Joe. 'So I walked over and I was like, "Oh, I love those magazines!" and I walked away. They were freaked out!'

Famous fans

As well as the millions of ordinary kids who adore the Jonas Brothers, the band also have some famous people among their followers, including Beyoncé, Emily Osment, Miley Cyrus, Billy Ray Cyrus, Akon, Perez Hilton, as well as President Bush himself (who recently admired Joe's shoes!). American TV star Kim Kardashian has also confessed that she loves the Jonas Brothers, saying she thinks Nick is particularly cute! Between them, the brothers have quite a list of famous friends too: Aly & AJ, Miley Cyrus, Everclear and Chelsea Staub to name but a few!

'It's awesome to have my brothers on stage and in the studio with me. You have a security that everything is going to be okay, even when you mess up.'
Nick

Rumours!

Of course, one of the pitfalls of being famous is all the rumours, which focus mostly on their female friends! But the Jonas brothers are grounded and don't let it get to them – in fact, they think it's funny. 'I heard that I was dating all of the swimsuit models in the world ... at the same time!' says Joe.

One thing the boys find difficult is when they do something embarrassing in public. Nick says that the worst for him is when he's flying, because he sleeps all the time when he's on planes and his mouth falls wide open – he thinks he looks totally stupid! He's woken up to find tweens staring and taking pictures of him looking like that. Poor Nick!

'I've fallen off stage before. I didn't get hurt, but I jumped back on stage and acted like I was supposed to fall!'
Kevin

Camp Rock!
And other TV appearances

'They're hilarious, they're awesome, they're like my brothers, they're complete gentlemen and professionals – they're cool.'
Demi Lovato on the Jonas Brothers

They may well have been writing songs and touring for the past few years, but the Jonas Brothers' biggest impact so far is the big-screen Disney smash: *Camp Rock!* The movie – which is set to be an even bigger smash than the *High School Musical* series – features all three Jonas Brothers, with Joe taking the leading role.

CAMP ROCK: THE STORY

The movie is a Cinderella tale with a modern day twist to it. It is centred on the story of a teen girl, Mitchie Torres (played by Demi Lovato), who has an amazing singing voice and desperately wants to attend a prestigious summer rock camp. Her family can't afford to send her, but realising how much her daughter wants to go, Mitchie's mother gets a job as a cook there and takes Mitchie with her, on the condition that she helps out in the kitchen between classes.

Mitchie is befriended by fellow camp member Caitlyn (played by Alyson Stoner), and spends her time living a double life at the camp: posing as a well-off camper and hiding the fact she is the cook's daughter. Her secret is discovered, but when she is overheard singing (but not seen) by teen pop star

'The biggest challenge of doing the movie was acting in general. It's so new to us. We're so used to performing onstage. I didn't know how I would do. Honestly, I got kind of nervous! But I felt really comfortable about halfway through.'
Joe

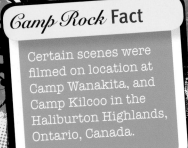

Camp Rock Fact

Certain scenes were filmed on location at Camp Wanakita, and Camp Kilcoo in the Haliburton Highlands, Ontario, Canada.

and celebrity camp instructor Shane Gray (Joe Jonas), he is completely taken and sets out to find the girl behind the beautiful voice. Meanwhile, Mitchie will have to learn how to confront her fears, step out of the kitchen and into the spotlight as herself.

THE JONAS CONNECTION

Although Joe takes the leading role, there's enough of Kevin and Nick to keep Jonas Brothers fans happy! 'I wanted to see more of my brothers in the movie, too, because they were so good in it,' says Joe. Nick points out that doing their first movie 'was an extreme opportunity' they were excited to have.

All three brothers agree that the one thing that drew them to the movie was the music. 'We listened to the songs. We thought the music was something that was really interesting to us. Especially the song we did as the band Connect Three. That's maybe a song that we would do one day. So it all kind of worked out. It was good!' says Nick. The movie's spectacular soundtrack is sure to have you bouncing around your room and practising those dance moves all year long!

CHARACTERS

Shane Gray (Joe Jonas) has the male lead role of the movie. He is the lead singer of the band, Connect Three, who originally met and formed at Camp Rock. Now a successful rock star, Shane messes up by storming off the set of a music-video shoot. His band Connect Three cancel their summer tour and send him to rock 'n' roll camp to get his bearings and find himself again.

The other two band members are Nate and Jason (Nick and Kevin Jonas), who – in the movie – aren't related at all, unlike in real life! Nate (Nick Jonas) is Shane and Jason's best friend and fellow band member. He is the guitarist and vocalist of Connect Three. Nick's character is sort of bossy – like Nick in real life, says Joe!

Jason (Kevin Jonas) is the lead guitarist of Connect Three and his character is not too bright – Kevin is hilarious at playing an airhead!

CAST

Joe Jonas as Shane Gray
Demi Lovato as Mitchie Torres
Meaghan Jette Martin as Tess Tyler
Nick Jonas as Nate
Kevin Jonas as Jason
Alyson Stoner as Caitlyn
Anna Maria Perez de Taglé as Ella
Jasmine Richards as Peggy
Aaryn Doyle as Lola

OTHER TALENT

The movie features a whole gang of talented tween stars that are sure to hit the same stardom as the cast of *High School Musical*: among them, Demi Lovato, Alyson Stoner (*Cheaper by the Dozen*), Meaghan Jette Martin, Anna Maria Perez de Taglé (of Disney Channel's *Hannah Montana*), Jasmine Richards (*Naturally Sadie*), Maria Canals-Barrera, Daniel Fathers, Roshon Fegan, Jordan Francis and screenwriter/actress Julie Brown. Phew!

Camp Rock Fact

While the brothers were in Canada filming *Camp Rock!* Nick had a day when his blood sugar was a little out of control; he says he was 'kind of bumming. I walked by this room in the hotel we were staying at, and it was so weird, all of a sudden there was this big ballroom with a piano in it. It was like a scene out of a movie. So I went in there, sat down at the piano and wrote the song. Later on I played it for the cast and they all loved it.'

'My character is out there, a little spacey, but I love it. I get to be a little loopy, and it's kinda fun. Nick plays the leader in the group, which is really true. He always keeps me in line – me and Joe are always goofing around. I'm always just having a good time; Joe is goofing off.'
Kevin

ON-SET

The Canadian set where the movie was filmed was so beautiful, according to the boys, that they fell in love with it. 'We'd sneak into one of the boats and take off or sit on the dock and hang out. It felt like we were really at camp!' says Joe. The brothers definitely made friends with their fellow cast members. Joe says of co-star Demi Lovato: 'She is fun, very mature and always there when you need someone. Plus she's a supercool friend and a great singer!'

As soon as the filming for the movie was over, the cast really missed each other – just as if they had actually gone home from summer camp! Meaghan Jette Martin (who plays bratty rich kid, Tess Tyler) says 'the cast members are all such great people. I definitely miss them the most.' When the cast were on set they might have been spending some time in front of the cameras – but Meaghan says they mostly hung out in school, because they all had to do school first thing in the day for three hours!

Camp Rock's *Message:*

'Stay true to who you are.'

37

TV APPEARANCES

As well as the smash hit that is *Camp Rock!* the Jonas Brothers have also done their share of TV, appearing on *Ellen*, *Entertainment Tonight* and *Oprah* (where staff received 5000 emails from fans pleading to have the boys on the show!).

LIVING THE DREAM

The boys were also filmed for a reality TV show for the Disney Channel, called *The Jonas Brothers: Living The Dream*. The show follows the life of the band as they prepared to embark on their first headline tour around North America, the *Look Me In The Eyes* tour. The show features clips of the band rehearsing, travelling, performing, studying, and at home with their family and friends. Fans share the experiences with the Jonases on the tour bus, as they rehearse and perform, go sky-diving and race go-carts!

J.O.N.A.S!

As if all this wasn't enough, the Jonas Brothers are also set to star in a new television series: *J.O.N.A.S!* (Junior Operatives Networking As Spies). The boys will all play themselves, and the concept is three brothers living double lives: one as rock stars and the other as spies! The Jonas Brothers all play themselves, and Chelsea Staub co-stars. In this world of darkness and evil, these three brothers, with the help of their secret agent dad, must thwart the evil deeds of Dr Harvey Fleischman, an evil dentist bent on taking over the world's young adults!

However, thwarting evil and saving the world can be difficult when you're also going to high school, keeping your secret identity from Mom, and being stalked by Stella Malone, a teenage reporter working undercover who's trying to get the behind-the-scenes scoop! This is sure to be a hit – keep your eyes on those screens for more hot Jonas Brothers action!

Nick's on-set embarrassing moment:

'I think sometimes when you forget your lines, it's kind of a funny moment. There's one scene where I was supposed to be saying something like "By the way, we told the press you'd be singing a duet with the winner at Final Jam" and it came out like "By the way, winter's coming faster than summer so make sure you wear some pajamas" or something like that. It was crazy!'

Fashion
and style

From the get-go, the boys have always rocked the latest trends. Whether they're playing to a sold-out crowd of thousands of screaming fans, appearing on *Oprah* or just chilling with friends, you can be certain you'll see the brothers wearing some cool threads.

Style is really important to the boys. Every day they dress up, putting on ties and wearing J. Lindeberg and Marc Jacobs. They like the high-fashion rock look. In fact, the only sweatpants Joe owns are Adidas Velour! 'You totally would see us in things like blazers, skinny ties and sparkly shoes even when we're not on stage,' says Kevin, 'We like to dress up, and that was part of our goal. We always said we wanted to bring some high fashion back to rock 'n' roll!'

> 'I love gold, I love socks, I love to wear socks all the time.'
> **Joe**

Natural Nick

While touring, Nick guards his socks. At home, he keeps count of the socks in his drawer.

Nick's favourite piece of clothing is a Yankees hat.

Nick's trademark is his curly hair.

Nick keeps his closet surprisingly clean.

Nick's most prized wardrobe section is his tie collection.

Nick once bought a hat that cost $1,550.

Each member of the Jonas Brothers has his own individual style too:

Nick likes to call his style 'formal rock' and says rolling up your sleeves is key! 'I like to be a little more dressed up,' says Nick. 'I guess you could call it preppy, but I call it formal rock.' And an interesting hair fact: Nick's trademark curly hair actually used to be straight! When he turned 12, it turned curly. 'It was the weirdest thing in the world,' he says. 'It's always been kind of long, but when it gets really long I want to cut it all off. My mum, dad and manager are always like, "You have to keep your long hair!"'

Joe says his look is 1990s, 80s, 70s, 60s, 50s, 40s because he likes to incorporate everything. And he's a known fashion icon these days: at a charity event, President Bush was sitting near the Jonas Brothers and gave Joe respect for his style. 'The President liked my shoes!' says Joe. 'His wife was talking, and he leans over and goes, "I like them shoes, Joe. I gotta get me a pair!"' Now that's a snappy dresser!

Kevin aims for an almost Victorian dandy style with collars. He likes wearing suits and he has to have shiny shoes all the time, even with sweatpants, which his brothers always tease him about! Despite leaving his clothes all over the bedroom he shares with brother Joe, Kevin doesn't like wearing a shirt twice. 'I hate not having clean clothes. If I have a shirt and I've worn it, it needs to be cleaned. I'm really weird about it!' says Kevin.

Jazzy Joe

Joe's most prized possession is his hair (he uses straighteners and products to achieve his look).

Joe sometimes wears glasses because he is short-sighted.

Joe's first big purchase was a pair of Nike Dunks.

Joe's trademark is his headband.

Joe has red starry socks which he wears for luck.

Joe's 'choppy locks' hairstyle is inspired by Japanese manga cartoons.

Joe's favourite tie is his zebra-striped one.

Kool Kevin

Kevin's favourite pieces of clothing are his Nike shoes.

Kevin buys too many shoes when shopping (he likes boots).

He doesn't like to wear shirts twice, and he's not afraid to wear pink shirts.

Kevin's trademark is his bandanas.

Kevin's bad habit is leaving clothes everywhere.

Kevin can't wait to come out with his own fashion line.

Jonas Brothers
fashion fact

All of the boys' clothes for their tours are made with rip-away buttons, because they have to undergo costume changes in two minutes!

SLICK STYLIN'

Even if you're born with rock-star talent, it can take some help to get that look just right! The Jonas Brothers' stylist, Michelle Tomaszewski, started working with the band back in 2006 and has helped them shape their look from distressed jeans and sneakers into their current mode of 'aristocratic rock stars'. Thankfully, the boys were eager to embrace their new look, and now they get excited when they go shopping.

'Nick can't stand it if someone wears his socks, he flips out and it's so funny.'
Kevin

Girls, Dating, Love

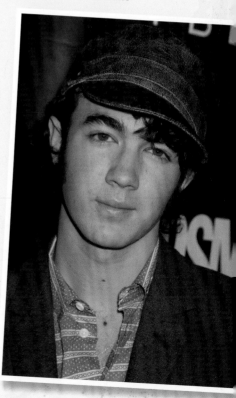

KEVIN JONAS – MR EXPERIENCE

Being the oldest, Kevin's had the most experience with girls. But he still knows the limits: all three brothers wear promise rings to symbolise that they are waiting for the right girl. Oldest bro Kevin has been wearing his since he was 16 years old, but it fell off when the family was on holiday in the Bahamas. 'I was like, "Oh, man, this is not cool,"' he says. 'Joe and Nick were still wearing their rings. I got the exact same one again!' Because of the rings, a lot of people ask whether the boys are married, which of course they aren't. But being the cool customers they are, the brothers don't really like to talk about their romantic status.

Relationships

Kevin is a relationship guy. He doesn't believe in dating lots of different people. Once, when Kevin asked a girl on a date, she immediately thought he was her boyfriend. 'But that's not the way it's supposed to be. Relationships take time,' says the wise Jonas brother. When he sees a girl he likes, he gets a nervous feeling in his stomach, which is how he knows he really likes someone. He's also learned to listen to what other people have to say about his crushes. 'I have dated a girl that my brothers didn't like, and it ended terribly. They were right, and now I listen to what everybody has to say,' he says.

'I look for a girl who's cool. Like we just hang out and not see me as a "celebrity". I don't like it when girls run up and say "I'm totally in love with you". There's no mystery there. I mean from fans it's great, but from a girl you're gonna date ... it's different.'
Kevin

47

As the boys are always away on tour, long-distance relationships are the only option. Kevin says that long distance is hard work but if it's meant to be, then it will work out. 'The hardest aspect of a relationship is maintaining it,' he says. 'Girls are always a big test, but one thing I've learned is to keep trying!'

Positive qualities

The first thing he notices in a girl is her confidence level. 'I like someone who will be real and talk to me. It's also cool to have a good conversation with a girl. And I love a good smile.' He says that the girl's heart is important, and it's essential that she has a good attitude. As for hair colour, he says that he is a sucker for blondes and redheads but usually the smile gets him right away, and that's how he can tell if they're a genuine person or not.

Kevin is very relaxed – he can watch movies for hours at a time – so he likes a girl who's easy-going, makes him laugh and who likes to be constantly connected. Because he's rarely home, he likes to keep in touch with someone via email, texting, or on the phone (if it came to it, he'd rather call a girl than text). He says it's nice to be able to turn on his computer and see his girl's buddy icon pop up. When he really likes a girl, Kevin can't stop talking about her! And he doesn't get nervous holding hands with a girl. 'Actually,' he says, 'it kind of stinks when I want to hold her hand and she's like "Not so much."'

Just a normal guy

While you might think that superstars don't get nervous about going on dates, think again – when Kevin is around a girl he likes, he sweats! He's also really afraid of getting

Kevin: Crush Facts

First kiss: When Kevin kissed a girl for the first time, he missed her mouth.

Second date: 'I'll know if I want to ask a girl on a second date in the first ten minutes of our first date. If you're just getting to know each other and you're already laughing about things in each other's lives, then you know you're going to work out.'

On break-ups: 'Break-ups, in general, are always bad. Some break-ups are easier than others, but sometimes they're really hard. You learn to get through it. That's why I think love takes time and definitely should not be rushed into.'

On love: 'I believe in love at first sight.'

Advice for guys: 'Guys should still open a door for a girl every chance they get, every time. They should try to take care of a girl as much as possible. She's like a princess, no matter what.'

Celebrity crushes: Kevin's celebrity crushes are Jessica Alba, Hayden Panettiere, Brenda Song, Hilary Duff and Miss America (Lauren Nelson). If Kevin's mum Denise could pair Kevin up with any one celebrity it would be Hilary Duff, because, she says, 'she's such a sweetheart!' Today, his major celebrity crush is girl group Girls Aloud!

Pre-date preparation secret: Before a date, both Joe and Kevin straighten their hair!

rejected by girls. 'I have to remind myself that although it may be risky, I'm doing what I love. I also know that if you don't take chances, then you'll never know what will happen!' Kevin has always been a people-pleaser. But look out girls – he's trying to be less of a pushover, and making an effort to voice his opinion more!

Kevin's date no-nos

He doesn't like it when a girl is constantly complaining about how she looks. He also hates it if a girl talks on her phone all the time when she's with him. He also says it's not cool if a girl has a foul mouth, or if her friends are crazy or odd, because if that's who she's hanging out with, it definitely rubs off on her. He says the most annoying thing a girl could do is text on her phone during the entire date.

Bad dates!

Being the oldest, Kevin has loads more embarrassing date stories than his brothers. 'One time I took this girl out to eat at a really nice place in LA,' he says. 'We ordered a ton of food, but when the bill came, I realised I'd forgotten my wallet! My dad had to bring it to me. It was so embarrassing! I didn't think it was big deal, but Nick and Joe still tease me about it!' Once Kevin had a girlfriend who would send back the notes he had written to her with all his spelling errors circled – which really bummed him out!

The perfect date

As a guy who has flown across the country to see his crush, Kevin is no stranger to romance. Once, on Valentine's Day, he wrote a letter to a girl, burned all the edges and rolled it up, then he put it inside a bottle and painted everywhere she wanted to go on it. He melted a candle down on top of it and had it waiting in her room. So thoughtful, sigh!

To try and make a girl feel special, Kevin will try to surprise her, like by showing up completely unannounced with Starbucks coffee. Because he's not around too much, he also calls as many times as he can (without being weird!).

Ultimately, Kevin just wants a girlfriend who has a positive attitude and is easy-going – like him – and who also understands his crazy schedule!

'For me, music is just life in general. When you walk outside, you start hearing beats everywhere you go.'
Kevin

JOE JONAS – MR LOVER LOVER

Out of all the Jonas Brothers, Joe is the biggest ladies' man. So, it's no surprise that one of his favourite days is Valentine's Day, even though a girlfriend once dumped him on it! Joe's also been on blind dates before. And once he sent a big bouquet of flowers to a girl he liked who lived in a foreign country. Joe's not shy about letting a girl know he's into her, but he doesn't like girls to ask him out – he prefers to make the moves. When he's with a girl he likes, he usually gives her hugs and nudges and flirts with her – without even knowing it! To be funny, when people ask about his promise ring he jokes that he's married. But actually it's a promise he takes seriously. 'My ring is basically a part of me. It's cool!' he says.

The Perfect Girl

The first thing heart-throb Joe notices about his crush is her eyes – he's totally an eyes guy. He likes a girl to have natural beauty – he isn't into girls who wear a lot of make-up. Fashion-wise, he likes it when girls wear leggings. 'I like girls who have a cool sense of fashion and don't mind standing out a bit,' he says. Joe also thinks that looks aren't as important as attitude. He likes girls who like to have fun, especially if they're talented. In his opinion, every girl has something special about her. According to Joe, the best thing a girl can do to show she cares about a guy is to support what he likes to do, so keep turning up to those shows! He also likes girls to write him letters. But at the end of the day, a girl has to pass the biggest test of all: Joe's parents must like her too. 'If Mom likes a girl, then it's all good,' he says!

The Chase

If there's one thing that ladies' man Joe loves, it's flirting! He's all about keeping it fun and light-hearted. He thinks you should keep it playful for as long as you can – that's way better than immediately telling your friend, 'Hey, tell him I like him.' In Joe's opinion, that completely kills it. Joe thinks it's a lot of fun when he can't quite tell if someone likes him or not. It drives him crazy!

Perfect Date

Joe's been on some crazy dates, as you might imagine. One Halloween he went trick-or-treating all day with his crush, and had an awesome time, but they ate too much candy and both wound up getting sick! Joe likes doing fun active things on dates, so something like bowling would be perfect for him. He'd also like a girl to blindfold him and take him to Disneyland. His best date outfit includes his zebra tie or his Hong Kong Mr Lee custom-made suit and Dior shoes. When he gets ready, he steals some things from Kevin's closet, maybe a little from Nick's too. Well, that's what brothers are there for!

Joe: Crush Facts

About his brothers: 'If a girl didn't like my brothers, I'd probably be like, "Peace". I would give her the peace sign and walk away. My brothers are my boys. How can I be your boy if I can't have my boys?'

The Guy Code: 'Best friends don't date each others' ex-girlfriends. That's just how it rolls. It's the guy code.'

Favourite pick-up line: 'You're like my library card 'cause I'm checkin' you out!'

First pick-up line: In kindergarten, Joe didn't know what to say to the girl he liked, so he blurted out, 'I like your red marker!'

Out to lunch: 'I wish I would have known that going out with a girl to lunch on a date is not a good idea. It automatically puts you in the "friends zone"!'

On bad dates: 'If a first date is going badly and you're out to dinner at a fancy place, you have to wait for your meal to come out. It's a better bet to go to a fast-food joint. This way if it's a bad situation, at least the food comes out really fast!'

The perfect kiss: 'Guys just want to kiss you, not your make-up, so too much lip gloss is not a good idea! Kisses are perfect in front of a sunset. And I think it's better to be alone if it's your first kiss in a new relationship. Everyone else doesn't need to see it.'

Bad Dates

As if being dumped on Valentine's Day wasn't bad enough, Joe also shared a New Year's kiss with a girl – only for her to break it off the next day! Another time, he went to see a movie with a girl and a creepy old lady followed them everywhere they went. He says he doesn't think she was a fan or anything, but it freaked him out!

Celebrity Crushes

Joe's celebrity crushes are Emma Watson, Jessica Alba, Katharine McPhee and Natalie Portman. If Joe could trade in his brothers for any other celebrities, he'd trade Kevin for Shakira and Nick for Beyoncé. Joe once dated Amanda Michalka (from pop sensations Aly & AJ). The reason for their break-up was the distance between them. He has also been romantically linked with pop singer JoJo and Chelsea Staub. Just what you'd expect from the ladies' man of the Jonas Brothers!

NICK JONAS – MR COOL

Cutie Nick – the youngest of the brothers – has his fair share of admirers, but he's quite picky when it comes to the sort of girl he likes. 'I know that true love is definitely out there,' he says. He used to rush into relationships a lot, but that didn't work too well. Now he takes it slow, and makes sure he spends time getting to know the girl first, which he found works better. But, he says, 'If it's really awesome, I'll still jump into it!'

'Sometimes it is about either what is going on in my life right now, or how we are feeling that day. A lot of the songs can be really happy when we are having a great time, but some songs will be very sad.'
Joe

Nick's first celebrity crush was Miley Cyrus, and he is rumoured to have dated her in the summer of 2006. He laughs off the gossip about his love life, saying 'I just think it's funny. Because you take a picture with somebody, everybody automatically assumes you're dating!'

Good qualities

The first thing Nick notices in a girl is her eyes. And he really loves dresses on a girl. 'I like a girl who looks like a lady,' he smiles. 'Like, I would get dressed up for prom, so it will be sweet if my date came dressed up too.' But Nick likes girls to be dressed appropriately. 'Some girls try too hard to get guys' attentions by not wearing many clothes,' he says. 'When a girl dresses nicely with good taste it says that she has confidence and that she takes pride in her appearance.'

Other qualities Nick looks for in girls include confidence, and he also likes someone who has a lot of energy because he's not that energetic, though he has had crushes on girls who are quiet too. He hates it when a girl is afraid to eat in front of him, and he would never date a girl with a bad attitude. 'Because I'm Mr Positive!' he beams.

Hi-tech dating

Nick says he would rather text a girl than call her, because sometimes when

Nick: Crush Facts

On love: 'I know I've been in love, but I waited a long time before I said the word "love" to someone even though I'd been thinking it, because I consider "love" to be more than just a word,' he says.

Model behaviour: Nick's parents have given him a great example of what love is, and he's also learned a lot from his brothers. 'I've learned a lot about dating from my brothers. I've done really well with the relationships that I've been in so far.'

Celebrity crushes: Miley Cyrus, Jordan Pruitt, Anna Kournikova, Brenda Song and Camilla Belle.

First kiss: Nick's first kiss was really good! 'It was looking over the city skyline. It was sweet! It was awesome.'

Pick-up line: 'Slow down, sugar, because I'm a diabetic!'

On flirting: Nick says that boys don't really know what they're doing half the time. 'Sometimes I'm oblivious to flirting, and I just have to ask, "Okay, what's the deal? Are you into me or not?" Or I'm the last one to even realise that I have a girlfriend until someone mentions it.' Nick's also cautious when flirting because he says that it's a dangerous thing, as you never know if someone is flirting with you or just giving you a compliment.

he calls a girl his heart starts beating really fast and he gulps nervously! How cute! 'When you're texting, you can say things to a girl that you'd never say in person. You just type what you want and press send,' he says.

But he also gets embarrassed when texting: 'It's embarrassing for me to text message back and forth with a girl – I'm asking all these questions just to continue a conversation when I should just be hanging out with her!'

Although Nick has never had a girlfriend during Christmas-time, he says the perfect holiday date scenario would be Christmas in New York City. He says he'd like to go to Central Park, hang out by the ice-skating rink, and possibly go to the Rockefeller Center. 'A date should be about having fun!' he says. 'You should be able to share everything with your girlfriend.'

Up close and personal

Nick also has a tendency to look away when he starts to like a girl. So if he has to try hard to look in her eyes and be engaging during a conversation, then he knows it's for real! And he's a really considerate boyfriend: 'I usually don't do one huge thing that's really nice. I like to spread little gifts out here and there,' he says. His favourite way to impress a girl is by singing to her – and who could refuse an offer like that!

Nick acts in two different ways when he's around girls – sometimes he's really quiet, but other times he's the complete opposite, telling jokes and clowning around. How he acts depends on the girl. 'It helps when a girl's really confident because then I don't feel like I have to entertain her,' he says. 'What I'm looking for in a girl is someone who will understand my crazy schedule and will be there to support me. Just a girl who will make me smile and keep me happy.'

Looking to the Future

Well, it's definitely been a rollercoaster ride that's brought the Jonas Brothers to where they are today! From singing in the church choir to playing at sell-out stadiums to thousands of screaming fans, these three boys from New Jersey have come such a long way. 2008 has seen them release their third album, perform on a sell-out headline tour, play across Europe supporting megastar Avril Lavigne, star in a smash-hit Disney movie and record their own TV series, *J.O.N.A.S!*

'There are a lot of places we have never been, and we can't wait to see and meet all the new people!'
Kevin

But rather than letting all this success go to their heads, Kevin, Joe and Nick remain the down-to-earth cuties we know and love. Kevin says: 'We've kind of grown up with the saying, "Even if you're at the top, live like you're at the bottom".' In typical Jonas fashion, these brothers are always looking to the future, focusing on what they can do better and all those things they have yet to achieve! As Kevin says: 'This is just the beginning. We've got to keep working hard, keep busting our butts and trying to make it go one step further. It is just the beginning for us.'

Although they might be making their move to the big screen, these are three boys with music in their blood. In fact, if their musical career wasn't such a groundbreaking global success, the brothers say they might have thought about studying music at Berklee School of Music. But as it is, the shining talents of these three brothers mean they are the

perfect stars for stage, movies and TV. Joe — who always wanted to be a comedian when he grew up — is really excited about acting. 'I'd love to be a comedian,' he says. 'I've always loved to make people laugh. I would love to do more comedic roles in movies one day.'

Nick's also hoping for him and his brothers to do more acting, among other things. 'We hope to continue making music and touring, and I think we'd love to do more acting. We'd like to write and produce for some other artists too, so we'll see what the future has to hold. We just hope we can carry on doing what we love.' Seeing as Kevin, Joe and Nick have become such hot property, the brothers are bound to have countless offers to see them through the next few years!

One thing is for sure — we won't see any solo projects just yet. The boys are such a tight-knit unit that they all want to keep collaborating for years to come. Joe says: 'We're brothers so it's not like if we got upset at each other we can be like, "Well I quit." They're still my brothers. We love to do this and we know we're going to keep doing it for a very long time.' So we can all breathe a sigh of relief, safe in the knowledge that there's going to be a lot more Jonas Brothers action to come. Watch this space!

'There's definitely a little bit of Prince in the new record.'
Joe

PICTURE CREDITS

GETTY: 2, 3, 6, 9 (top right), 10 (left), 12 (top right), 14, 20, 22 (bottom), 24 (top), 26 (left), 27, 28-29, 31, 33, 37 (right), 41 (left), 42, 43 (left), 51, 52 (right), 54 (left), 55 (left), 57 (top), 60-61, 63

REX FEATURES: 4, 5, 7, 8, 9 (bottom left), 10 (right), 13, 15, 16 (bottom left), 17, 19, 21, 23, 24 (bottom), 30 (top) 34-35, 37 (left), 38-39, 40, 41 (right), 43 (right), 44, 47, 48-49, 50, 52 (bottom), 54 (bottom), 55 (right), 57 (bottom), 58

PA PHOTOS: 11, 12 (bottom left), 16 (top left), 18, 22 (top), 25, 26 (right), 30 (bottom), 32, 36, 45, 46, 59

ACKNOWLEDGEMENTS

Posy Edwards would like to thank Helia Phoenix, Amanda Harris, Anna Valentine, Helen Ewing, Rich Carr, Kate Oliver, Daniel Bunyard, Alexandra Towle and Sophie Buchan.

First published in hardback in Great Britain in 2008 by Orion Books
an imprint of the Orion Publishing Group Ltd
Orion House, 5 Upper St Martin's Lane,
London WC2H 9EA
An Hachette Livre UK Company

1 3 5 7 9 10 8 6 4 2

ISBN: 978 1 4091 0160 4

Design: www.carrstudio.co.uk
Printed in Canada

The Orion Publishing Group's policy is to use papers that are natural, renewable and recyclable and made from wood grown in sustainable forests. The logging and manufacturing processes are expected to conform to the environmental regulations of the country of origin.

Every effort has been made to fulfil requirements with regard to reproducing copyright material. The author and publisher will be glad to rectify any omissions at the earliest opportunity.

www.orionbooks.co.uk